Seven

a novel by

ANTHONY BRUNO

based on a screenplay by
Andrew Kevin Walker

Level 4

Retold by Ron Veness
Series Editors: Andy Hopkins and Jocelyn Potter

Pearson Education Limited
Edinburgh Gate, Harlow,
Essex CM20 2JE, England
and Associated Companies throughout the world.

ISBN: 978-1-4058-8230-9

First published in Great Britain by Bloomsbury Publishing Plc 1995
This adaptation first published by Penguin Books 1997
Published by Addison Wesley Longman Ltd and Penguin Books Ltd 1998
New edition first published 1999
This edition first published 2008

5 7 9 10 8 6

The moral right of the adapter and of the illustrator has been asserted

Typeset by Graphicraft Ltd, Hong Kong
Set in 11/14pt Bembo
Printed in China
SWTC/05

Published by Pearson Education Ltd in association with
Penguin Books Ltd, both companies being subsidiaries of Pearson Plc

Contents

Introduction

"There are going to be five more murders if we don't find the killer."
With Mills leading the investigation after his retirement, Somerset
had a feeling that the killer would do them all, no trouble. It wasn't
that Mills was no good. He just didn't know anything about this sort
of stuff – about serial killers.

Detective Somerset has just seven more days before he retires.
He is looking forward to leaving the city and living peacefully
away from the city. Maybe he will meet someone and have
children. Maybe, at forty-five, he is not too old to become a
father. After twenty-three years as a homicide detective in the
city, he has seen enough crime. He does not want to see any
more senseless murders. He only wants to get through these last
seven days as easily as possible. But with about sixty homicides
a month in this city, he is not going to have a very easy week.

At the next murder scene, he meets Detective David Mills,
a younger man who is new to the city. He has left his job in a
small town because he wants to do work that he thinks matters
more. Somerset thinks that he is a fool for coming to the city.

The next morning, a very fat man is found dead in his
kitchen. Then Eli Gould, the city's top criminal defense lawyer
is killed. There are clues left by the murderer. Is this the work
of a serial killer? What do the clues mean? It does not take
Somerset long to understand. This killer plans to murder seven
people – one for each of the Seven Deadly Sins. Can they find
him and stop him before he murders again?

The Seven Deadly Sins are a Christian idea, introduced by
the Roman Catholic Church. They became part of early

Christian teaching when the Church decided that there were two types of sin: those that are less serious and seven that are very serious. The "seven deadly sins" became a popular idea in Christian art and were written about by the famous Italian poet, Dante Alighieri (1265–1321). These seven sins are Pride, Wrath, Envy, Lust, Gluttony, Greed, and Sloth. These words are explained on the page after this Introduction.

The movie *Seven* came to the movie theaters in 1995. It was made by David Fincher, who made pop videos before working in movies. Fincher's first big movie was *Aliens 3* (1993). Both *Aliens 3* and *Seven* show a very dark view of people and the world they live in. In *Seven*, the city has given Somerset such a dark view of life that he doesn't believe in having children. The dark rooms and the rain in the movie add to this feeling as we watch it. The movie was mainly filmed in downtown Los Angeles and in the Mojave Desert, but the name of the city is never reported in the book or the movie, so it could be any US city. Morgan Freeman played the tired, middle-aged Detective Somerset, and Brad Pitt played the younger and more enthusiastic Detective Mills. While working on the movie, Pitt broke his arm, and so this was written into the movie (see the picture on page 31). He earned $4,000,000 for his work, which probably made him feel better. Gwyneth Paltrow, famous for her part in *Shakespeare in Love* (1999), played Mills's wife, Tracy. Kevin Spacey played John Doe, the killer. It is one of the best-made movies of the 1990s.

Andrew Kevin Walker wrote *Seven* for the movies. He graduated from Pennsylvania State University in 1986, where he studied Film and Video. While working in a music store in New York City, he wrote this story about two detectives and a serial killer. It took him three years to write it. When he finished, he sold the story to a movie company in Los Angeles. Walker also played the dead body in the movie's opening scene. He went on to write the movies *8MM* (1999) and *Sleepy Hollow* (1999).

Anthony Bruno wrote the story of *Seven* from the movie. Bruno, an American, has written several other books about crime, including *The Iceman*, which is a true story about a serial killer in the US. Bruno is married and lives in New Jersey with his wife and daughter.

Violence in American cities has entertained movie-goers for many years, and serial killers are a great subject for a detective movie with plenty of terror. This dark and frightening story is fiction, but there is something very real about it at the same time. The older detective wants to leave this terrible city and start a new life in a safer place. He knows he cannot save the city from the criminals and now he just wants to save himself. The young detective wants to make changes and make the city safer for everybody. But this society is controlled by greedy and cruel people and it needs more than one or two men to change it. The serial killer wants to send a message to humanity. But is this the work of a mad man? The innocent wife of the young detective finds herself living in fear and does not believe that her husband has made the right decision. Is she right? There are only seven days to find out.

The Seven Deadly Sins

A SIN is something bad that God has told people not to do. The *seven deadly sins* are the most serious sins that only God himself can forgive.

Pride is the sin of being too proud.

Wrath is the sin of being too angry.

Envy is the sin of wanting things that belong to other people.

Lust is the sin of wanting a thing or a person – often sexually – very strongly.

Gluttony is the sin of eating and drinking too much, often in an unpleasant way.

Greed is the sin of wanting to have too many things – too much money, for example – for yourself.

Sloth is the sin of being very lazy.

Chapter 1   Gluttony

Somerset looked at the clock. It was almost 2 a.m. He had been in bed for more than an hour, but he was still awake. He had too much to think about. After twenty-three years as a homicide detective, it was never easy for him to go to sleep.

A homicide detective sees humanity at its very worst. He sees murders of every imaginable sort. People killed with guns, knives, poison. Husbands killing wives, and wives killing husbands. Children killing parents, friends killing friends, and people killing strangers. Sometimes to rob them, sometimes for no reason at all.

But now Somerset was leaving. He had only seven more days left before he retired. Then he could leave the city, forget the crime he had seen, and live quietly in the country.

He had seen enough of the violence and crime of the city. His pictures and his books were packed and ready to move to his new house in the country.

Only seven more days. He thought of how long he had lived in the city. He had been married twice. At one time he had wanted to have children—but not in the city. He knew what living in the city did to children. But deep in his heart, he felt that it wasn't right not to have children. It isn't too late, he thought, forty-five isn't too old to have children. He still might meet someone. It was possible. Anything was possible once he got the hell out of here.

Suddenly his stomach was tight. Was he making a mistake? He'd lived his whole life in the city. What if he hated the country? He tried to stop himself thinking and go to sleep. It will all be OK, he told himself. Only seven more days of crime, of the noise and mess and violence in the city, and then his life would start all over again.

That afternoon he had visited the house he was buying in the country. The house was old and needed some fixing, but he liked it.

On the way back to the city, he sat on the train and watched the farms and fields go by. But the countryside became drier and the farms turned into desert. Soon he began to see burned cars out there on the dry, empty land. He knew they were getting close to the city.

Somerset could see smoke and dust hanging over the city like the hand of an angry God. When the train stopped, he didn't want to get out. He wanted to stay in his seat until it took him back to his new home. But it was only seven days, he told himself. He could manage another seven days. After twenty-three years, what is seven days?

Out on the street, as he waited for a taxi, the terrible reality of the city hit him hard. The noise of the traffic, people running, shouting, screaming, and nobody caring.

A crazy, homeless man was trying to take a tourist's suitcase. "I'll get you a taxi," the crazy man shouted. "I know how. I'll get you one." But the tourist, whose wife and daughters were afraid, didn't want his help. They didn't want him there. Somerset was going to help, but he couldn't do it. He couldn't be responsible for everything if he was ever going to escape this place. People had to solve their own problems.

He got into a taxi and told the driver to take him home. On the way they passed an ambulance and two police cars. Somerset could see a body on the sidewalk. He saw the bloody face and wondered if the man was still alive. On the next street a fight began. A crowd stood around the fighting men, shouting. As they passed, Somerset sat back in his seat and closed his eyes. He didn't want to see any more.

"Where did you say you're going?" the driver asked. Somerset opened his eyes. "Far away from here," he said.

◆

Yes, he thought. *Far away from here.* He closed his eyes, and started to breathe more deeply...

In the morning the phone woke him from a deep sleep. There had been another murder. As he got out of bed, he wished he didn't care as much as he did. It would make the next seven days a lot easier.

◆

When Somerset arrived at the crime scene, the workers from the police department were taking photographs and looking for fingerprints. The body was on the floor in a body bag,* waiting to be taken out. There was a lot of blood on the wall, and a gun on the floor next to the body.

"The neighbors heard them screaming at each other," said a policeman. "The man who lives in the back said it was going on for about two hours, which wasn't unusual with these two."

A young man with short hair and a black leather jacket came into the room. "Detective Somerset?" he asked. "I'm David Mills. Today's my first day on homicide."

Somerset shook his hand, but said nothing. Mills watched him walking around the room. Somerset was a thin, middle-aged black man with heavy bags under his eyes and a sad face. Everyone at the precinct had smiled when Mills said that he was going to start working with Somerset. Mills wondered why.

"Where was your last job?" Somerset asked him.

---

* body bag: a special bag to carry the bodies of people killed in crimes, accidents and war.

"Detective Somerset?" he asked. "I'm David Mills. Today's my first day on homicide."

"Springfield. It's up north."

"How many homicides you get a year up there?"

"Oh, about sixty or seventy."

"We get that many a month here."

"Yeah, but we only had three homicide detectives up there." Mills didn't want to get into a fight in his new job, but he had left Springfield because he thought that it was too small and unimportant. He wanted to do real detective work. He wanted to feel that he was doing something that mattered.

Somerset thought Mills must be a fool for wanting to work in the city. "For the next seven days," he said, "I want you to remember that you're not in Springfield."

◆

Early the next morning, Mills was awake, sitting up in bed. Tracy, his wife, was asleep by his side. She didn't like the city, with its noise and dirt and crime.

Mills studied his wife's face. There was always something about Tracy's face—she had big eyes and a small mouth—that reminded him of a child. He thought that it made her more beautiful when she smiled. But she didn't smile so often now that they had moved to the city. Her face always looked worried. Even in her sleep she worried.

Maybe this move is a big mistake, thought Mills. Maybe Somerset is right. Maybe Springfield *is* a better place.

No, he thought. He was right to move. But he was happy that Somerset was retiring. He understood why everyone at the precinct wanted him to go.

The phone rang. Tracy jumped up. "What is it?" she cried.

Mills picked up the phone before it rang twice. "It's OK," he said. "It's only the phone."

It was Somerset. "Meet me at 377 Baylor Street," he said. The way he spoke annoyed Mills.

"What've we got?" he asked.

"Possible homicide," said Somerset, and hung up before Mills could ask anything more.

♦

Outside the apartment block on Baylor Street, Somerset was already waiting when Mills arrived. "We'll need some lights," said Somerset. "The electricity is off inside."

"Any guess about the time of death?" Mills asked Somerset.

"No, but it seems he's been sitting with his face in a plate of *spaghetti* for forty-five minutes now."

Inside the apartment, there were dirty pots and dishes and

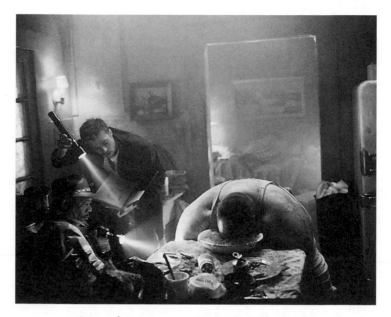

A very fat man was sitting at the table with his face in a plate of spaghetti. They had never seen anyone as fat as this man.

open cans and boxes of food everywhere, and there were insects feeding on the garbage. The smell was terrible. A very fat man was sitting at the table with his face in a plate of *spaghetti*. They had never seen anyone as fat as this man.

Somerset saw that his hands and feet were tied. He couldn't understand what had happened.

Then the Medical Examiner★ came into the room. He took no notice of the detectives.

"Do you think it was poison?" asked Mills.

★ Medical Examiner: a doctor who works with the police to solve crimes.

Instead of answering, the doctor lifted the man's face out of the *spaghetti*. "He's dead," he said. "We know that for sure. Point that light you're holding at his mouth."

"What do you see?" Somerset pointed the light and looked closer.

"There are little blue pieces around his mouth. See?"

"Yeah. So what is it, Doc?"

"Don't know. I never saw anything like that before." He let the man's head back down into the *spaghetti*.

◆

The dead man's name was Peter Eubanks. The body was in the Medical Examiner's room, where Mills and Somerset were talking to the doctor.

Eubanks had always been heavy, but not as heavy as he was when he was found dead: 304 pounds. The doctor said some of his bones were bending under the weight.

Mills wondered whether the man died of poison, but the doctor didn't think so. He explained why, showing Mills parts of the inside of the body, which was cut open for examination. Mills had to make himself look.

"Are you saying that he died from eating too much?" Mills asked.

"Yes. I think that's exactly how he died."

"What about these marks on the back of his head?" Somerset said. "It looks like a gun was pressed against his head."

"Very possible, if the gun was pushed hard enough against the skin."

Somerset was looking at a row of glass jars on a table. "Doctor," he said, "I want to ask you about one of these." He picked up a clear glass jar. "Were these blue things found around the victim's mouth?"

"No." The doctor picked up another jar. "These are the ones from around the mouth. Those you're holding I found in the stomach."

"Any idea what this stuff is?"

The doctor shook his head. "I have no idea." He covered the victim's body. Now he had more work to do.

"Four bodies came in this morning," the doctor said. "So we've been very busy here."

"Let me know as soon as you find out anything about this blue stuff, will you, Doc?" said Somerset as he went out.

◆

Back at the precinct house later that afternoon, the captain was sitting at his desk reading the papers on the "fat man" case. The victim no longer had a name. He was just "the fat man".

Mills waited while the captain read the Medical Examiner's report. The captain was about fifty, with big bags under his eyes and bad skin.

Mills could see that Somerset had worked hard on this case. He wondered what Somerset was really like. What would Somerset do when he was in danger? Would he think more quickly than Mills did on the night that Rick Parsons was . . .

Mills and Rick were old school friends. Rick was the best policeman they ever had in Springfield. But that night, when they were working on a murder case together, Mills thought that the murderer wouldn't shoot at the police. When Mills saw that the man had a gun, he hadn't fired quickly enough. He'd waited a little too long. The man fired at Rick, and now Rick would be in a wheelchair for the rest of his life. And no matter what Rick and Tracy said, Mills thought, he *was* to blame.

The captain was shaking his head over the papers. "This is very hard to believe," he said. "Do you believe it?"

Somerset nodded. "The victim had to choose. Eat or be shot. The killer put food in front of him, and made him eat it. Perhaps this went on for twelve hours or more. The killer kept him awake and made him keep eating."

The captain looked worried. Mills understood how he felt. He hadn't wanted to believe it either.

"I think this is just the beginning," said Somerset.

"We don't know that," the captain said sharply. "We have *one* dead man. Not four. Not three. Not even two."

"Then what's the reason for it?" Somerset looked tired.

The captain was angry. "Don't start, Somerset," he said. "Don't start imagining things before they happen. You have no evidence that there will be another murder."

Somerset was too tired to argue. "I want to be taken off the case," he said.

"You've only got a week left," the captain said. "What difference does it make?"

"This can't be my last case," said Somerset. "It'll go on and on. I don't want to leave it unfinished when I go. And, if you want my opinion," Somerset pointed at Mills. "This shouldn't be his first case."

Mills jumped up. "This isn't my first case!" he shouted. "You know that."

"This is too soon for him. He isn't ready for one of these," said Somerset.

"Look," the captain said. "I don't have another detective I can give this to. We don't have enough people. You know that."

"Give it to me, Captain," said Mills. "I can manage it."

The captain turned and stared Somerset in the eye. "You

serious about this killer? You think he's just getting started?"

Somerset closed his eyes and nodded.

"Hell!" the captain said. "As often as I've wanted you to be wrong, you rarely are. That's why I'm leaving you on the 'fat man' case, Somerset. As for you, Mills, I'm putting you on another case."

"But Captain . . ."

"Not buts. That's all. Now go."

Mills was so mad he wanted to throw a chair through the window. He wanted to stay with Somerset. He just didn't want them to think of him as a beginner. He wanted to show the captain that he could manage on his own. Even in the city.

"You heard me, Mills. Get going," the captain ordered.

Chapter 2   Greed

The next morning Somerset was in his office when the captain walked in.

"Have you heard?" the captain asked.

"Heard what?"

"Eli Gould was found murdered last night."

Gould was possibly the top criminal defense lawyer in the city. No criminal was too nasty for Gould to defend. If they could pay enough, he would do anything to defend them and help them escape punishment. It didn't matter how terrible their crime was.

"Someone broke into his office and killed him," the captain said. "They wrote the word 'greed' on the floor in his blood."

"Greed?" Somerset could think of worse things that could be said about Eli Gould.

"Someone broke into his office and killed him,"
the captain said. "They wrote the word 'greed' on the floor
in his blood."

"I'm putting Mills on the case. I told him he would soon have a case. I just wish it wasn't this."

Somerset went back to his typing. "I'm sure he'll do fine."

The captain was shaking his head and looking doubtful. "You won't like it out there in the country. You know you're not really leaving. You only think you can leave."

"I can't live here anymore," said Somerset. "I don't understand this place anymore. People used to kill somebody for a purpose, even if it was a stupid purpose. Now they do it for the hell of it, just to see what will happen."

The captain let out a deep breath. "I hear what you're saying.

11

It's just that I don't want to lose you. They don't make detectives like you anymore."

"You've got Mills. He'll be OK."

"But he won't be you."

Not if he knows what he's doing, Somerset thought.

"Oh, I almost forgot," said the captain, holding up a jar with the little blue pieces in it. "These were found in the fat man's stomach. The doctor thinks that the killer made him eat them. They're pieces of the floor."

◆

Somerset went back to Eubanks's apartment. He wanted to find where the pieces of blue floor had come from. He looked everywhere, but couldn't find anything until he felt under the front of the refrigerator. Then he could see that was where they came from. The larger pieces in Somerset's jar fit the holes. Someone had moved the refrigerator and broken pieces of the floor cover.

Somerset managed to pull the refrigerator away from the wall so that he could see behind it. The dirt on the wall was cleaned off and the single word GLUTTONY was written there. A clean, white envelope was pinned to the wall.

Somerset's blood froze. He reached for the envelope, but it was a little too far away.

◆

Later, in his now empty apartment, Somerset was thinking about what he'd found behind the fat man's refrigerator.

If he said nothing about it, there would be no link between the murders of Eubanks and Gould. Then it would be Mills's problem. But he couldn't do that...Mills wasn't ready for this. He thought he was, but he wasn't. It was still Somerset's problem. So now he had GLUTTONY and GREED.

◆

Mills was excited when he saw the note Somerset had found behind the fat man's refrigerator. "So we have a link between the two killings," he said.

He read the note again. *Long is the way, and hard, that out of hell leads up to the light.* "But what does it mean? Is he trying to tell us something? It just seems crazy to me."

It was hard for Somerset to control himself. But instead of telling Mills he was a fool, he held up photos of the words GREED, in blood, and GLUTTONY. "You ever heard of the seven deadly sins, Mills? Greed, gluttony, wrath, envy, sloth, pride, and lust."

Understanding slowly showed on Mills's face. "You think he's going to do one for each sin?"

"It seems so, doesn't it?"

"Oh, no . . ." Mills was shocked. "So we do have a link?"

Oh, no, is right, thought Somerset.

"You wanted the big time," he said. "Well now you've got it. There are going to be five more murders if we don't find the killer." With Mills leading the investigation after his retirement, Somerset had a feeling the killer would do them all, no trouble. It wasn't that Mills was no good. He just didn't know anything about this sort of stuff—about serial killers. This wasn't Springfield.

As much as Somerset wanted to leave, he couldn't. Not now. He couldn't just leave it with Mills. He had to go on with the investigation.

◆

Mills looked at his notes as he walked around Gould's office. On the wall behind the desk, there was a big oil painting. It was a modern painting, just lines and shapes of color—red, green, and black. On the desk, there was a weighing machine with dried blood on it. The letters in blood on the floor had turned red-brown.

Mills wanted to find some evidence, something that they had all missed. He wanted to show that Somerset wasn't the only one who knew how to do detective work. Mills believed that the crime scene was the place to solve the crime. There had to be some evidence, some clue, something that would help them find the killer.

He picked up a photograph of a middle-aged woman. She had a false smile, too much make-up, and colored red hair. It was Mrs. Gould. On the glass over the photo, the killer had drawn circles around her eyes in blood.

Was this a clue? Mills wondered. Why had the killer drawn these circles? Was she the next victim? Had she seen something? Or did the killer want them to see something? He couldn't understand it. What was it he couldn't see? Was it something so big and obvious that they were looking at it but couldn't see it?

◆

The next morning, Somerset was sitting at his desk working on the "fat man" case when Mills came in. Mills was carrying a pile of papers on the Gould case. He put it down on the desk and began studying photographs of Gould's office.

At first Somerset wanted to help him, but then he thought that Mills should learn to work by himself. He would learn finally, and Somerset was leaving in three more days.

In this case, though, people would probably die while Mills

14

was learning. He needed some help. Just to show him the right direction. Somerset put down his pen. "You know this is a serial killer we're looking for here," he said.

"You really think I'm a fool!" shouted Mills, angry at Somerset again.

"No, I didn't say that." Somerset was sorry he had said it the wrong way. "It's just that we haven't talked about that. I think we should."

"I don't."

"Why not?"

"Because as soon as we call him a serial killer, the FBI* will take over the case. Then we'll be working for them."

"But . . ."

"No," said Mills. "I don't even want to talk about it."

Just then the phone rang. It was Tracy, Mills's wife. She wanted to talk to Somerset, but Somerset couldn't imagine why.

"Detective Somerset?" she said. "I wondered if you would like to come and have dinner with us tonight."

"Well, that's very nice of you." Somerset's voice was uncertain.

"I'm a very good cook," she said. "And I've heard a lot about you. I would like to meet you before you leave."

◆

Later that evening, Mills seemed uncomfortable as he and Somerset walked up the stairs to Mills's apartment. Somerset knew that Mills didn't like the idea of dinner together, but he wasn't sure why.

In the dining room, the table was carefully prepared for three.

* Federal Bureau of Investigation. In the USA, national (not local) detectives.

A young woman came out of the kitchen. "Hello, men," she said quietly.

Somerset thought that she had a pretty smile, "Hello, Tracy," he said. "Nice to meet you."

"Please sit down," Tracy said. "Can I get you something to drink?"

"No, thanks. I'm fine just now." Somerset took off his jacket. He nodded toward the kitchen. "Smells good," he said.

Tracy was staring at Somerset's gun. He could see that it made her nervous. "I never wear a gun at the table," he said, taking it off. "It isn't polite."

Tracy tried to laugh. "You know," she said, "no matter how often I see guns, they still make me nervous."

"Me too," said Somerset, putting his gun into his jacket pocket.

"I hear you two were friends at high school," Somerset said.

"Yes," said Tracy. "I knew then that this was the man I was going to marry."

"So you're really an old married couple, if you count up the years," said Somerset.

"Yeah, I guess so," she laughed.

Tracy put a dish of *lasagna* on the table, and poured wine into their glasses. "Why aren't you married?" she asked as she sat down.

"I was married. Twice." Somerset looked thoughtful as he drank a little wine. "Somehow it didn't work, though."

"That surprises me," she said.

He laughed. "People soon find that I'm . . . not easy to be with," he said. "Just ask your husband."

Mills smiled. "He's right about that."

♦

"Why aren't you married?" she asked as she sat down.

Later, with the table cleared and Tracy asleep, Mills and Somerset were studying the photos of Gould's office.

"I think I'm missing something," Somerset said. "How do *you* think Gould was murdered?"

"Well, the way I see it, the killer got into the office before the building was closed on Friday. Gould's body was found on Tuesday morning. The building was closed all day on Monday, which means that the killer was probably with Gould all day Saturday, all Sunday, and even Monday."

Mills picked up a photo of Gould's body in the high-backed leather chair. "Gould was undressed and tied up," he went on. "But one arm was left free. Now, the weighing machine on the desk that didn't belong to Gould. The killer brought it in. He gave Gould a sharp knife and made him cut out a piece of his body and weigh it. There was this

17

note," he picked up a photo and gave it to Somerset. "Look at this."

Somerset read the note: *One pound of meat, no more, no less* . . . His face was hard. "Saturday, Sunday, Monday. He wanted Gould to take his time. To sit there and think about it. What do you do when there's a gun in your face?"

"Right!" Mills picked up another photo. It showed the picture of Mrs. Gould with the eyes ringed with blood. "This is a photo of Mrs. Gould," he said. "If the killer's telling us she saw something, I don't know what it could be. She was out of town when it happened."

"What if it's not something she's seen, but something she could see, but she hasn't had the chance yet?"

"Yeah, but what is it she's supposed to see?"

Somerset shook his head. "Only one way to find out," he said.

◆

Mrs. Gould was in a "safe house", guarded by the police.

When Mills and Somerset walked in, Mills thought that it looked like a place where someone might go to kill himself.

Mrs. Gould was sitting on the bed, crying. "I'm sorry to come here so late, Mrs. Gould," Mills said. "But . . ."

"It's all right. I haven't slept since . . ." She began to cry again, holding her hand over her mouth as if to stop herself.

Mills took out the photographs. "Mrs. Gould," he said. "I need you to look at these again, and tell me if there's anything that seems strange or in the wrong place. Anything at all."

But she wouldn't look. "I've looked at them a million times," she said. "I don't want to see them again . . . ever."

Mills hated to see women cry, but he knew he had to do

this. "Please, Mrs. Gould. Anything at all. Take your time. Please . . ."

"There's nothing there," she said. She wouldn't look at the photos again.

"There's something there that we're not seeing," said Mills. "You're the only one who can help us now. We need your help if we're going to get the person who did this."

"All right," she said. She took the photos and started to look at them, but too quickly, Mills thought.

She stopped at one picture and looked again.

"What do you see?" asked Mills.

"The painting," she said.

The photo showed the desk with the big, modern oil painting on the wall behind it.

"What about the painting?" Mills asked.

She looked up at him as if he had done something wrong. "Why is it upside down?" she asked.

Somerset took the photo from the woman's hand, and looked at it. "Upside down?" he said.

♦

Mills and Somerset went straight to Gould's office. Somerset looked up at the painting. "You sure our people didn't move it?"

"Even if they did, the photos were taken first."

Somerset took the painting off the wall, Mills thought there would be another message behind it, written in blood. But there was nothing. "I don't want to think about the sleep I'm missing because of this," he said. "There's nothing here. He's playing with us."

Somerset thought that Mills was probably right. "But there

19

must be something here," he said. He was staring at the wall where the picture had been.

"What is it?" Mills asked.

"Quiet. I'm thinking."

This made Mills angry. Did Somerset think that he was really a fool?

Somerset took out a brush and a small box. Standing on a chair, he began to brush the wall with fingerprint dust.

"Do you know how to do that?" Mills was doubtful, but Somerset kept on working. Mills tried to be patient, but he wanted to see what Somerset had found. "What is it? What do you see? Nothing. Right?"

"Wait. Just wait," said Somerset, still working. Finally he moved away and Mills got a good look at what he had found.

Written in fingerprints, as clear as ink, was: HELP ME.

Mills couldn't believe what he saw. He looked at Somerset in surprise. *This guy really is good!* he thought.

Chapter 3   Sloth

Somerset needed to know if the fingerprints he had found matched those of a known criminal. He and Mills watched the computer operator as he began to search.

"I've known this to take as long as three days," the operator said. "So why don't you wait outside?"

Outside the computer room was an old sofa. Somerset sat down and looked at his watch. It was 1:20 a.m. Mills got a can of Coke from a machine and sat next to Somerset.

"You think our guy is crazy and asking for help? Is that his problem?" Mills asked.

Written in fingerprints, as clear as ink, was: HELP ME.

"No, I don't think so. It doesn't fit. I don't think he wants us to stop him. Not until he's finished."

"I don't know. There are plenty of people doing things they don't want to do because they have voices in their heads telling them to do bad things."

Somerset shook his head. "Not this guy. He may be hearing voices, but these murders were well planned. He's not going to stop until he's finished what he wants to do."

Mills said nothing. He drank some Coke, looking at Somerset.

"Something wrong?" Somerset asked.

"Why is it that nobody believes you're going to retire?"

Somerset didn't know how to answer this because sometimes he didn't believe it himself. Instead, he said, "You meant what you said to Mrs. Gould tonight about catching this guy, didn't you?"

"Of course."

"I could never say that to her. I've seen too many killers plead madness. The ones that can pay get a lawyer like Gould to defend them. And a lot just disappear. They kill for a few weeks or months, and then we never hear from them again. I can't think the way you do. That's why I'm going."

"If you think that, then what are we doing? Tell me."

"We just get all the facts, all the evidence. We write it down and hope that some day it will be used." Somerset knew that whatever he did, it rarely ended the way he wanted. In the end, twelve ordinary people decided whether a criminal was guilty or not guilty.

♦

"Wake up, sleepyheads! You have a winner!" It was the captain standing over them. Mills and Somerset had fallen asleep on the sofa. Mills looked at his watch. It was 6:25 a.m. *Never enough sleep*, he thought.

"Here's your man." The captain showed a photo to Mills and Somerset. It showed the thin face of a young man with long, stringy hair and lots of rings in his ears. Victor Dworkin was his name, age twenty-five.

"We know Dworkin. He's been in prison for robbery and sex crimes. The last time he was in trouble with the police, his lawyer helped him go free. That lawyer was Eli Gould. Mr. Greed."

Mills's eyes lit up. "That's our link!" he said.

"Wait. Nobody has seen or heard from Dworkin for months. But we do have an address, and we're checking it now."

A red-haired officer called California, and four other policemen in uniform, came running toward them. The captain began giving them their orders.

"What do you think?" Somerset asked Mills. "Is Dworkin our killer?"

Mills thought for a moment. "He doesn't seem like our man, does he? I don't see our killer fitting that description."

Somerset nodded. "No," he said. "Our guy seems to have more purpose. Dworkin looks like the type who has trouble getting out of bed in the morning."

"Yeah, but what about the fingerprints?"

Somerset took a deep breath. "Yes, they're his. So I suppose it must be him."

◆

Mills and Somerset were in their car, following the black police van taking California and the uniformed men to Dworkin's apartment. Somerset took out his gun and checked it.

Mills nodded at the gun. "You ever get hit by one?"

"A bullet? No. Twenty-three years on the job, and I've only taken out my gun three times. Never fired it, though. Not once." He put his gun away. "How about you?"

Mills shook his head. "Never got hit. Pulled my gun out once . . . And fired it."

"Yeah?"

"Yeah . . . It was my first time on something like this. The guy had killed his wife. I didn't think he was the kind who would shoot at the police. But when we broke through the door, he was holding a gun on a cop outside the window. He fired once. I fired five times."

"How did it end?" asked Somerset.

23

Mills thought for a moment. He changed the story a little because he felt so guilty. "I killed him. The other cop was hit in the leg." He wondered if he should tell Somerset what really happened to Rick that night.

"So how did it feel? Killing a man?"

"I thought that it would be bad. You know... But that night I slept well."

But that was only because he hadn't known about Rick then. Later, when he knew that Rick would never walk again, he didn't sleep so well. He still didn't.

Somerset was thoughtful for some time. Then he said, "Well, I've been lucky so far. I never killed anyone."

Mills just nodded. *Would today be like that night?* he wondered. Would Somerset get shot because Mills was too slow? *No way*, he thought. He wasn't going to let that happen again.

◆

The van stopped in front of them. This was Dworkin's apartment block. The uniformed police ran into the building. Somerset and Mills followed them in. Mills's mouth was dry. It had been just like this when Rick was shot. He pulled out his gun as they climbed the stairs.

On the third floor, they stepped over a man who was so drunk he couldn't move. Then they got to Dworkin's apartment.

California waved everyone back to make room for the two men breaking down the door.

"Move!" California shouted as the door broke open. "Police!" he shouted as he pushed through the broken door, holding his gun. "Police officers!"

When Mills finally got inside, he saw that the apartment

was small, dirty, and very dusty. The uniformed cops were everywhere.

"In here!" California shouted.

Mills moved fast to get into the bedroom first. There was a body under a dirty sheet lying on a small bed. California moved slowly toward it, his gun in both hands. Mills had both hands on his gun too. All he could think of was that Dworkin might have a gun under the sheet. He might shoot California just as Rick had been shot.

"Good morning!" California shouted.

The body didn't move.

"Get up!" California shouted again. "I said get up! Now!"

◆

Somerset looked in from the door. There was a terrible smell inside. SLOTH was written on the wall above the bed.

California lifted the sheet. Then everyone could see that Dworkin wasn't going to shoot. The body was tied to the bed. It was so thin that there seemed to be nothing but skin and bones. A bandage was tied over his eyes.

Somerset took out a photo of Dworkin. "Is it him?" Mills asked.

"Yeah. It's him."

California pointed with his gun at the man's right arm. The hand had been cut off at the wrist.

Mills kept shaking his head. He couldn't believe what he saw. "Oh, no, no," he was saying.

One of the policemen showed Somerset some photos pinned to the wall. They showed Dworkin tied to the bed. Each one had the date written under it, and in each one the body was thinner.

There was a terrible smell inside. SLOTH *was written
on the wall above the bed.*

"There are fifty-two of them," the policeman said. "I
counted."

Somerset pointed to the date on the first photo. "Exactly
one year ago today," he said. "What kind of man is this killer?"

Suddenly a loud noise came from the body. California
jumped back and fell over a chair. "He's alive!" he shouted.

Dworkin's mouth was open and his lips moved a little. A
strange sound came from his throat.

"He's alive!" said California again. "Get an ambulance.
Now!"

♦

Somerset and Mills were back in the office that afternoon. Somerset looked as if he had the weight of the world on his shoulders. It annoyed Mills. Somerset wasn't he only cop on this investigation.

"I want to catch him too," Mills said. "You know that. I want to *hurt* him."

Somerset picked up some papers. "Did you read this?" he asked. "The money for Dworkin's apartment was paid regularly. The killer planned and worked hard to keep Dworkin alive so long. Exactly a year to the day. And he paid for his apartment. He knows what he wants to do. And he's patient."

Somerset remembered the note he had found: *Long is the way, and hard* . . . And the seven deadly sins . . .? Somerset liked to read books. Perhaps the killer did too. That gave him an idea.

He took Mills with him to the public library. Somerset seemed to have friends everywhere. In a short time, he had a computer list of people who had borrowed books on subjects like crime, sin, the church, homicide, anything that would interest the killer.

They sat in Somerset's car and checked the list. Mills thought they were wasting their time.

"You got a better idea?" asked Somerset.

"Maybe this is one we should check," said Mills, suddenly sitting up. "This guy's had . . ." he counted. ". . . over thirty of these titles."

"What's the name?"

"You won't believe it," said Mills. "John Doe." *

---

* "John Doe" is a general name used to talk about the ordinary man in the street when you do not know his real name.

Somerset started the engine. "What address?" he said, as the car pulled into the street.

Chapter 4   John Doe

John Doe's apartment was on a narrow street in a poor part of the city.

They took the elevator to the sixth floor. Doe's apartment was in the front of the building, but Somerset thought that even if he had seen them coming, Doe wouldn't know who they were.

Mills knocked hard on the door. Somerset heard a noise, but it didn't come from inside the apartment. He turned and saw a dark shape in the shadow of a door.

Then he saw the gun. "Mills!" he shouted. They both hit the floor at the same time. The noise hurt Somerset's ears. Big holes appeared in the door of Doe's apartment.

Hollow bullets! thought Somerset. He imagined Mills getting shot. He would have to tell Tracy. But Mills had pulled his gun and run after Doe before Somerset could even think of stopping him.

Be careful, he thought. He was worried for Tracy.

Somerset followed Mills down the stairs. Doe was standing on the floor below, his gun in his hand. Mills jumped back just as Doe fired. The bullet hit the wall close to Somerset.

Mills waited for another shot. Instead he heard a door close. As fast as he could, he ran through the door and saw Doe running. Doe pushed a woman away and ran into her apartment.

"Police!" Mills shouted as he followed Doe into the apartment. He saw Doe climbing through a window onto the fire escape. Mills ran to the window. Doe fired again, breaking the glass. When Mills looked again, he couldn't see Doe, but he could hear him running.

Out on the fire escape, Mills ran and jumped to the ground. When he reached the street, he wanted to scream. There were people everywhere. In this crowd, he would never see Doe. Then, suddenly, impossibly, he saw him. Doe was waiting to cross the street, looking for a break in the traffic.

Mills ran straight into the street. Cars and trucks rushed past him, the drivers shouting at him.

Doe could see that Mills was following him. He ran through the traffic and disappeared into a narrow, dark street. Mills was close behind him, running fast.

Suddenly something hit Mills in the face. He dropped his gun—he heard it hit the ground—then he fell. The pain made him weak. *A board*, he thought, *a piece of wood*. He didn't see it coming, but that was all he could imagine. Doe had hit him with a board.

He was sure that his nose was broken. He was coughing blood. Trying to open his eyes, he saw a pair of legs and a hand picking up his gun. He tried to reach it and get it back, but the pain was too bad. Then he could feel his own gun pressed against his face. His mouth was full of blood. He couldn't see. He was helpless.

After a moment, the gun was gone. He was still alive. Then he felt something hit his chest. Then again, and again. Bullets. Doe was throwing the bullets at him. Emptying his gun.

He heard Doe running again, and began feeling for the gun and the bullets like a blind man.

"Mills!" It was Somerset running toward him. "You all right?" Somerset knelt down next to Mills. "I'll call an ambulance."

"No. I'm fine." Mills got to his feet.

"What happened?" Somerset wanted to know. But Mills was too angry to talk. He wiped the blood from his eyes and ran past Somerset as fast as the pain let him.

Somerset tried to keep up with Mills. Tried to get him to tell what had happened. But Mills was too angry. He was going to do something stupid. Somerset knew it.

◆

The broken door of Doe's apartment opened easily. Inside everything was dark because the walls were painted black. So were the windows. The living room had only a lamp and a chair in it. The next room they looked into was also painted black. There was one small bed with a dirty sheet on it. In the middle of the room was a small desk and a lamp. Inside the desk were neat rows of empty medicine bottles and boxes of bullets. Mills saw that some of the bullets were the hollow type that are called "cop killers."

In a corner of the room was a small table. On it there was a careful arrangement of things around a large glass jar. In the jar was a human hand.

Victor Dworkin, thought Mills. *Oh, man . . .*

Mills found the bathroom. It had only a soft red light. Doe had made it into a photographic darkroom. Film hung all around. Photos were pinned to the wall everywhere. There were pictures of Peter Eubanks, still alive; Eli Gould cutting into his own body; Victor Dworkin, his face asking the camera for pity. There were also pictures of a blond woman sitting on a bed. She wasn't hurt, but she looked very uncomfortable.

Mills could see how much work and preparation Doe put into his killing. There were also photos of Somerset and Mills at Dworkin's apartment.

Mills found the phone in the bedroom. He picked it up.
"Hello," he said.

Suddenly a phone rang. Mills ran out of the bathroom. Somerset was running the other way. "Where is it?" he said.

Mills found the phone in the bedroom. He picked it up. "Hello," he said.

Nothing. Someone was there, but he wasn't saying anything. Mills said "Hello?" again.

"I admire you," said a thin voice finally. "I don't know how you found me. I admire you detectives more every day."

"OK, John," said Mills. "Tell me . . ."

"No, no, no! You listen to *me*. I'll have to change my plans now. I just had to call to say how clever I think you are, and to apologize for hurting one of you."

Mills was really angry, but he didn't answer.

"I'd like to say more," Doe went on. "But I don't want to spoil the surprise."

"What do you mean, John?"

"Until next time," said Doe.

"John! Wait . . ."

But Doe was gone.

In another room Somerset discovered John Doe's "library".

Three of the walls were covered with books. The same kind of books that Doe had borrowed from the public library. Somerset wondered how Doe found time to read them all. One wall was covered with Doe's notebooks. There were thousands of them. Each one with about 250 pages, all filled with Doe's own writing, and with photos and pictures cut from magazines.

Mills thought that these notebooks were crazy, but Somerset disagreed. He thought that they were horrible but interesting. Doe's writings frightened Somerset, but he spent hours reading the notebooks, trying to understand Doe's thinking.

Doe didn't like all the horrible things that people had to live with these days. Somerset agreed with Doe about a lot of this. That was why he wanted to retire and live in the country. But Doe wanted to change things. The problem was that Doe was also horrible. Murdering people couldn't make anything better.

Mills came into the room where Somerset was reading. "Does he say anything about the murders?" he asked.

"No, I haven't found anything yet," said Somerset. "Do you have anything new?"

Mills showed him a photo of a blonde woman standing on

a street corner. "There are pictures of her in the bathroom, with other pictures of Doe's victims."

Having your picture taken by Doe wasn't a good sign. "any idea who she is?" asked Somerset.

Mills shook his head. "Whoever she is, she caught Doe's eye."

"Better check it with the office," said Somerset. "Maybe they know who she is. Perhaps we'll get lucky and find her while she's still breathing."

Somerset looked at his watch. It was past eleven. "Better go home now and get some sleep," he said.

Chapter 5   Lust

An hour later, Somerset was lying in bed when the phone rang. It was Tracy.

He looked at the clock. It was after midnight. "Tracy, is everything all right?" he asked.

"Yes, yes. Everything's fine. I'm sorry to call you so late. I just . . . I need to talk to someone. Can you meet me somewhere? Maybe tomorrow morning?"

"I don't understand, Tracy," said Somerset. "You sound worried."

"I feel really stupid, but you're the only person I know here."

"I'll help you if I can, Tracy," he said. He couldn't imagine what he could do for her.

"If you can meet me tomorrow, call me. Please. I have to go now. Good night." She hung up.

♦

The next morning Somerset met Tracy in the Parthenon Coffee Shop near the precinct house.

"So what's on your mind, Tracy?" he asked.

"You know this city," she began. "You've been here a long time. I haven't."

Somerset nodded. "It can be a hard place," he said.

"I haven't been sleeping well since we came here. I don't feel safe. Even at home."

He didn't know what to tell her. Maybe she should talk more with her husband. "Talk to him about it," he said. "He'll understand."

"I don't know why I asked you to come," she said. Her hands were shaking. "You know that I'm a teacher," she went on. "I've been trying to get work in some of the schools here. But the schools are ... horrible." She was starting to cry.

"What's *really* worrying you, Tracy?" he said.

"I ... I'm going to have a baby."

"Tracy," said Somerset. "I'm not the one to talk to about this."

"I hate this city," she said.

"If you're thinking ... ," he let out a long breath. "... about whether to have the baby ... "

"But I *want* to have children," she said.

"All I can tell you, Tracy," he said, "is that if you don't keep the baby, if that's what you decide, never tell David. But if you're going to have it, tell him now. That's all the advice I can give you."

Tracy took his hand as he got up from the table. "Promise you'll keep in touch after you retire. Please."

"Sure. I promise," he said, and waved good-bye from the door.

As Somerset reached the precinct house, Mills met him at the door. "We've got another one," he said.

Somerset felt tired and empty. But he wasn't surprised. He knew it was going to happen again.

♦

The outside of the Hot House Massage Parlor was painted bright red. Police cars were parked everywhere out front. Uniformed cops were trying to control the crowd of confused people, but they weren't having an easy time.

Mills pushed through the crowd with Somerset just behind him.

A cop was trying to talk to the doorman. "Did you hear any screams?" he asked. "Did you see anything that seemed strange?"

"No," said the man. He was a big, fat man, who looked like an ugly animal. "Everybody who comes in here looks strange. And they're screaming all the time in there. That comes with a place like this."

"You like working in this place, man?" the cop asked. "You like the things you see?"

There was an ugly smile on the man's face. "No, I don't," he said. "But that's life. Right?"

Mills and Somerset pushed past the crowd of people. Inside, the walls were painted red, and the red lights made it more red. The red light and the beat of the heavy-metal rock music reminded Mills of a scene from hell.

"Detectives?" A confused cop led them to a room with a strong light that went on and off quickly. "They're in there," said the cop, stopping at the door. "But I don't want to go in there again. I'll wait right here."

Mills stepped carefully into the room. He was confused by

the light. The music was just as loud in there. Two medical workers were trying to calm a man with no clothes on. He was about fifty-five years old, with dark gray hair. His hands were tied behind his back. On a large bed in the middle of the room was a body covered with a sheet. There was a lot of blood on the sheet. Some of the victim's blond hair hung over the edge of the bed. It made Mills think of Tracy, and that made him angry. Why did anything in this hell make him think of his wife?

"He made me do it!" the gray-haired man shouted, fighting with the medical workers. "He had a gun!"

The word LUST was written on the wall over the bed. Mills was so angry when he saw it that his hands were shaking.

Somerset was looking at the body. "You won't want to see that more than once," warned the medical worker.

"He had a gun!" shouted the suspect again. "He made me do it!"

Mills was looking over Somerset's shoulder. What they saw made them feel sick. There were no marks on the top part of the body—but lower down . . .

"He asked me if I was married," said the suspect. He was quieter now. "He had a gun in his hand . . ."

"Where was the girl?" Somerset asked.

"The girl? W-w-what do you mean?"

"Was she on the street?"

"S-s-she was on the bed. S-s-sitting on the bed."

"Who tied her down?" Somerset asked. "You or him?"

"He had a gun, a gun . . ." The man was starting to cry. "He had the gun in my mouth!"

Mills remembered the taste of the gun in his own mouth after Doe had hit him in the face. His stomach was turning

36

over. He took out his notebook and turned to the page where he had written the seven deadly sins.

Another one down, he thought, his hands shaking. *Three more to come. Envy, wrath and pride.*

He looked at the blood on the sheet. *What next?* he thought. *Holy God, what next?*

Chapter 6   Pride

The phone woke Mills. He sat up suddenly. Tracy's nails were digging into his arm. "David! What is it?"

Mills picked up the phone quickly. "Hello?"

"*I've done it again.*"

Mills's blood turned to ice. He knew that voice. It was John Doe. How did he get Mills's number?

"Doe! Are you there? Talk to me!"

But it wasn't Doe. It was Somerset.

Mills was angry. "What's wrong with you, Somerset?" he shouted. He looked at the clock by the bed. It was 4:38 in the morning.

"I just got a call from the officer guarding Doe's apartment," said Somerset. "Doe called there and left the message you just heard."

"Is that all he said?"

"Yes. We also found another body. Pride."

Tracy looked worried. "David," she said. "What's happening?"

Mills's head was hurting. "I wish I knew," he said.

◆

When Mills arrived at the new crime scene, the police department workers were already busy. Somerset and the Medical Examiner were in the bedroom. The first thing Mills saw were the words on the wall over the bed: PRIDE—then underneath—I DID NOT KILL HER. SHE WAS ABLE TO CHOOSE.

Sitting up in bed was the body. Her face was bandaged. There was blood on the bandage. In one hand she held a small bottle. Two red pills had fallen out onto the bed. The bed was crowded with soft, woolly animals.

The doctor started to cut through the bandages around her head. Mills was afraid of what he was going to see.

Somerset had found a photo of the victim. He showed it to Mills. Her name was Linda Abernathy. She was beautiful.

The doctor took off the bandage. Her nose was gone. Mills had to look away. His stomach was turning over. He had to leave the room.

"The killer cut off her nose," said Somerset, "and gave her the bottle of pills. She could choose to live without a nose or kill herself."

◆

Mills and Somerset drove back to the precinct house through the slow-moving traffic.

As they got out of the car, a man got out of a taxi and followed them into the building.

"Excuse me. Detective?"

Mills kept on walking.

"Detective?"

Mills turned around, and almost fell over with surprise. It was John Doe. Doe smiled and held up his hands. His shirt and pants were wet with blood.

By this time, Mills and several other cops had their guns pointed at Doe.

Mills couldn't believe this was happening.

"It's him!" California suddenly shouted. He pulled his gun and ran up to Doe. Pushing his gun against Doe's ear, he shouted, "On the ground! Now! Move!"

By this time, Mills and several other cops had their guns pointed at Doe.

Somerset ran back down the stairs. "Be careful!" he shouted. Doe was lying on his face, doing what he was told, but Mills wasn't going to take a chance. He stood over Doe with his gun pressed against Doe's neck. "Hands behind your head!" he ordered. "Don't move!"

Doe turned his head and smiled at Somerset. "Hello," he said.

California shouted "Shut up!" and pushed Doe's head to the floor.

"What is it?" whispered Mills to Somerset. "I don't understand this."

Somerset could only shake his head.

Doe looked at Mills again. "I want to speak to my lawyer," he said.

Chapter 7   Envy and Wrath

Somerset watched through the glass as Doe talked to his lawyer. Doe was calm and smiling. He looked like any ordinary man. He didn't look like a killer.

Doe's lawyer was asking questions and taking notes. Somerset couldn't hear what they were saying because the rules of American law won't let anybody hear what a criminal says to his lawyer.

Mills and the captain watched over Somerset's shoulder. "When can we question him, Captain?" asked Mills.

"You can't. Because he's saying he did it, it goes straight to the public lawyer's office."

Mills shook his head. "He wouldn't just say he did it. It doesn't make sense. He doesn't feel sorry. Look at him."

"He's not finished yet," said Somerset.

The captain laughed. "What can he do in prison?"

"I don't know. But I do know he's not finished yet. He can't be. He's still got Envy and Wrath to go before he's finished."

"Maybe he's already finished. We just haven't found the bodies yet."

"I don't think so," said Somerset. "He likes sending messages. Why would he keep quiet about the last two?"

◆

That afternoon, Mills and Somerset were called to the captain's office. Doe's lawyer, Mark Swarr, was there.

The captain nodded to Swarr. "Tell them," he said.

Swarr turned to the two detectives. "My client has told me that there are two more bodies—two more victims, hidden. He says he will only tell where they are to Detectives Mills and Somerset, and only at six o'clock today."

"Why us?" Mills asked.

"He says he admires you."

"This is all part of his game," said Somerset.

"My client also says that if you don't take his offer, he will plead madness and the bodies will never be found. If you do take his offer, he'll plead guilty to all the murders right now."

"If your client pleads madness," said Somerset, "what you're saying would show that he isn't mad."

"Perhaps," said Swarr, "but think of what the papers would say if the police didn't try to find the bodies of two of his victims."

"If there really are two more bodies," said Somerset. He knew that it was wrong to do what Doe wanted. But he couldn't see any other possibility.

◆

Mills and Somerset sat in a police car on the precinct parking lot. John Doe was in the car with them.

A mile away, California and two cops with guns waited in a

helicopter. As the helicopter lifted into the air, a uniformed cop gave Somerset the sign to move.

Somerset and Mills had microphones on them. California would be in the helicopter, listening to everything that was said. If anything went wrong, he would be right there.

Somerset drove through the city streets until they left the buildings behind. Twenty minutes later, they were on the freeway, driving through the desert.

♦

"Stop here," Doe said. "This will be fine." Somerset slowed down. There was nothing but desert. Further along the road was a long, low building. That was all they could see.

Somerset stopped the car. Doe looked at Mills. "Can we get out now, Detective?" he said.

Mills and Somerset looked at each other. It was hard to know if this was part of the plan or just madness.

Somerset looked for the helicopter, but he couldn't see it. He couldn't imagine what Doe wanted to do here. They were in the middle of nothing, but if anything happened, the helicopter would be there like a cat on a mouse.

Doe was looking back down the road. "What time is it?" he asked.

"Why?" said Somerset. "What are you looking for?" He looked at his watch. It was just past seven.

"It's close," Doe said. "It's coming."

In the distance, a white van was coming along the road toward them, making a cloud of dust.

Somerset took out his gun. "Stay with him," he shouted, and started running toward the van.

Mills pulled his gun and held Doe more tightly. "Wait!" he

shouted at Somerset. But Somerset kept going. Mills put his gun to Doe's face. "Don't move!" he said.

♦

California tried to hear what Somerset was saying. There was a lot of noise on his radio.

"*Delivery van...*" he heard. "*Don't know what...*" Did Somerset need him or not?

♦

Doe was strangely calm. "It's good we have some time to talk," he said, and began walking toward Somerset.

"Down!" ordered Mills, pushing Doe to his knees. He kept his gun pointed at Doe while he watched Somerset.

Doe turned his head back. He was still smiling calmly. "I envy you, Detective," he said.

Somerset fired a warning shot into the air. The van stopped quickly. "Get out!" he shouted at the driver. "Get out with your hands over your head. Now!"

The driver got out, hands high. "Don't shoot me!" he cried. "What do you want? Just tell me. I'll give you whatever you want!"

"Who are you?" Somerset kept his gun pointing at the man. "What are you doing out here?"

"I'm working. I'm delivering something."

"Who to?"

Somerset kept his gun to the man's head as he opened the back of the van. "It's that one," the man pointed to a box. "This strange guy gave me five hundred dollars to bring it out here, at seven o'clock exactly. I'm a little late, but..."

"Get it out on the ground," Somerset ordered. "Slowly."

The delivery man put the box on the ground and stepped back, his hands on his head.

Somerset saw that DETECTIVE DAVID MILLS was written on the box.

♦

California could hear Somerset through the noise. "*There's a box here, it's from Doe...Don't know what...Going to open it.*"

"Call the bomb department," California told the pilot. "Get them out here quick."

"Should I go down?" asked the pilot.

"No. Wait. He hasn't asked us yet."

♦

Mills tried to see what Somerset was doing. The delivery man started to run. Somerset was chasing him away, ordering him to run.

Doe was still talking. "I wish I was an ordinary man," he said. "I wish I had a simple life."

Somerset was on his knees, doing something in the road. "What's going on?" said Mills to himself.

Somerset took out his knife and began to open the box. Inside was something heavy with plastic sheets around it. There was blood on the plastic. He looked inside.

'Oh, Christ..." He fell back onto the ground, suddenly weak. Not wanting to look. But he had to look. "Oh, Christ, no..." He felt sick.

Mills could see that something was wrong. He pulled Doe by the shoulder. "Get up! Stand up! Let's go!"

Doe tried to walk, but he couldn't move fast enough for Mills.

"There's a box here, it's from Doe . . . Don't know what . . ."

"You've made a good life for yourself, Detective . . ."

"Shut up and walk!" ordered Mills angrily.

Somerset took deep breaths to keep himself from falling. His legs were weak. He held onto the van, his stomach turning over. When he looked up his eyes were full of tears, and he couldn't see clearly, but Mills and Doe were coming toward him. "Oh, God, no, no . . ."

"Somerset," Mills shouted. "What the hell is going on?"

"Throw down your gun!" Somerset shouted.

"What are you talking about?" Mills shouted back.

Doe was still talking. "I'm trying to tell you how much I admire you . . . and your pretty wife, Tracy."

Mills turned around fast. "What did you say?"

Doe was smiling.

Somerset ran up to Mills. "Throw down your gun! That's an order!"

"You're retired!" said Mills. "I don't have to listen to you." He moved closer to Doe, his gun pointed at the killer's chest.

"I visited your home this morning, Detective," said Doe. "You weren't there. I tried to play husband. Tried to be a simple man . . . but it didn't work. I took something with me though."

Mills's face showed his pain and confusion. He turned to Somerset for some answers.

Somerset held out his hand. His eyes filled with tears. "Give me the gun," he said.

"I took something to remember her by," said Doe. "Her pretty head. I took it because I envy your ordinary life, Detective. It seems that Envy is *my* sin."

"It's not true!" screamed Mills, pushing his gun in Doe's face. "Say it! It's not true!"

Somerset pulled Mills away. "I can't let you do this, Mills."

"What's in the box, Somerset? *Tell me!*"

Somerset couldn't say the words.

"I just told you, Detective," said Doe calmly.

"Shut up!" Mills shouted.

"Become *Wrath!*" Doe wanted to make Mills more angry.

"Shut your mouth!" Mills hit Doe across the face with his gun.

"This is what he wants, Mills. Can't you see that?"

"Kill me, Detective."

"He wants you to do it," said Somerset. "Don't do what he

"Kill me, Detective."
"He wants you to do it," said Somerset. "Don't do
what he wants. Murder a suspect, Mills, and you throw
everything away."

wants. Murder a suspect, Mills, and you throw everything away."

"We'll say he tried to run, and I shot him. We'll work out the details later. No one has to know."

"They'll get you, Mills. They won't care who he is. A cop who kills a suspect can't defend himself. Forget about it. You'll go to prison."

"I don't care."

"If you're gone, Mills, who's going to fight the fight?"

"Don't listen to him," said Doe softly. "Kill me!"

"You're wrong," Somerset argued. "Who will take my place if you're not here?"

"Tracy pleaded for her life, Detective. And for the life of the baby inside her."

Mills looked confused. His hands holding the gun were shaking wildly.

"You didn't know?" Doe looked shocked.

Somerset was suddenly tired and weak. "If you kill him, Mills, he wins."

Doe closed his eyes, his hands held together in front of his face.

"Ok . . . he wins." Mills fired the gun, and the top of Doe's head flew off as he fell backward. Bloody pieces lay in the dusty road.

Mills dropped his gun. He turned and started to walk, but only took a few steps before he fell to his knees, holding his face in his hands.

Somerset looked at the body. A pool of blood spread from what was left of Doe's head. Somerset closed his eyes. He didn't want to see anymore.

◆

Two hours later Somerset was still there. There was a circle of police cars with their headlights shining on the crime scene. They had taken Mills away more than an hour ago.

The captain walked over to Somerset. "It's over," he said. "Go home."

"What happens to Mills now?" Somerset asked.

"We'll get him a good lawyer, but he'll go to prison. No doubt about that."

"So Doe did win. He got seven. Eight, if you count Mills.

Nine actually, if you count the . . . baby." Somerset had a hard time saying it.

"Go home," the captain repeated. "You're retired now."

"I've changed my mind. I'm staying. I don't want to retire."

"Are you sure?"

"I'm sure." He opened his car door. "See you Monday," he said. He knew he could never leave now. With Mills gone, someone had to stay to fight the fight.

ACTIVITIES

Chapter 1

Before you read

1 Look at the Word List at the back of the book and then answer these questions.

    a If a *homicide* detective is looking for a *serial killer*, does he question *suspects* or the *victims*?

    b When the *cops* find some *clues* at a crime scene during an *investigation*, do they use them as *evidence* in the court later?

2 Read the Introduction and answer these questions. What do you learn about:

    a the difference between Detective Somerset and Detective Mills?

    b the serial killer?

    c the Seven Deadly Sins?

3 Study the words and their meanings on the page before Chapter 1. Which sin are these people guilty of?

    a A person who thinks he/she is a better person than other people.

    b A person who will do anything to get more and more money.

    c A person who allows himself/herself to be controlled by sexual desires.

    d A person who eats much more than he/she needs.

While you read

4 Which of these describe Detective Somerset? Put a (✓) next to the correct sentences.

    a He wants children but does not want them to live in the city. .....

    b He is retiring and buying a house in the desert. .....

    c He cares about his job very much but wishes that he didn't. .....

d He is well liked by everyone at the precinct. .....

e He thinks that the fat man's murder is only the first
of many. .....

f He is the captain's best detective because he is
rarely wrong. .....

5 What do you know about the dead man? Are these sentences
true (T) or false (F)?

a His hands and feet are tied and his face is in a plate
of *spaghetti*. .....

b His name is Peter Eubanks. .....

c He has weighed 304 pounds for many years. .....

d He was probably poisoned, the doctor thinks. .....

e Blue things are found around his mouth and in his
stomach. .....

After you read

6 What does Somerset feel or think about these? Why?

a retiring

b the way the fat man was murdered

c this case

d putting Mills on the case

7 What do you know about the relationship between:

a Mills and his wife, Tracy?

b Mills and Rick Parsons?

c Mills and Somerset?

8 How would these people describe Mills, do you think?

a Tracy **b** Somerset **c** Rick Parsons **d** the captain

Chapter 2

Before you read

9 In your opinion, what does Mills care most about? Will he make
a good husband to his young wife and a good detective? Why
(not)?

10 Read the title of Chapter 2 and look at the picture on page 11.
What do you think will happen next? Why?

11 Match the two parts of each sentence. Write 1–5.

    a Eli Gould would defend the worst criminals   .....

    b The captain shows Somerset a jar with little blue pieces .....

    c The murderer made the fat man eat pieces of the floor from under the refrigerator and   .....

    d After Somerset shows Mills the note from the killer   .....

    e Somerset knows that Mills   .....

        1) he has to tell him the names of the seven deadly sins.

        2) that were found in the fat man's stomach.

        3) has no experience of serial killers.

        4) if they paid him enough.

        5) he wrote the word GLUTTONY on the wall.

12 Circle the correct word in *italics* in each sentence.

    a In Gould's office, Mills notices a weighing machine with *blood / money* on it.

    b The killer has used blood to draw circles around Mrs. Gould's *eyes / smile* in the photograph.

    c *Mills / Somerset* does not want to call the murderer a serial killer because the FBI takes over those cases.

    d Gould's killer tied him up, leaving one arm free. He made Gould cut out pieces of his *body / notes* and weigh them.

    e When Mills and Somerset go to Gould's office, Somerset discovers the killer's next message written in *ink / fingerprints*.

After you read

13 What do you think? Why has the killer:

    a killed Eli Gould?

    b written GREED on the floor in Gould's blood?

    c put circles of blood around the eyes of Mrs. Gould in the photo?

    d chosen to make Gould slowly kill himself over three days?

    e turned the painting upside down?

    f written HELP ME in fingerprints?

14 Work with another student. Have this conversation.

Student A: You are Tracy and it is the morning after you invited Somerset to your house for dinner. Talk to your husband about Somerset and about the dangers of working in the city.

Student B: You are David Mills. Tell Tracy about Somerset. Explain why your job is so important to you. Try to make her feel safe and happy with your new life together in the city.

Chapter 3

Before you read

15 Discuss these questions.

    a What do the clues left by the killer tell the two detectives about him?

    b Why do you think the killer leaves these clues?

    c What does Somerset understand that Mills does not?

    d Will they catch the killer before he murders more people, do you think?

16 Look at the picture on page 26. What do you see? What do you think is going to happen next?

While you read

17 Put these events in the correct order. Write 1–7.

    a Mills tells Somerset that he wants to catch and *hurt* the killer.   .....

    b Somerset and Mills take the fingerprints to a place where they will be matched against the fingerprints of known criminals.   .....

    c The detectives learn that the fingerprints in Gould's office belong to one of Gould's criminal clients.   .....

    d Somerset looks at the killer's photos of Dworkin, showing that he began his terrible treatment of him exactly a year ago.   .....

    e The police find Dworkin tied to the bed with a
       bandage over his eyes and his hand cut off.   .....

    f Somerset tells Mills that he has been lucky –
       because he has never killed anyone.   .....

    g California breaks down the door to Dworkin's
       apartment, and the police officers enter.   .....

18 What do you know about the killer? Tick (✓) the correct
sentences.

    a He paid Dworkin's rent and lived with him.   .....

    b He patiently kept Dworkin alive, planning the
       exact date of his death.   .....

    c He cut off Dworkin's hand so he could use his
       fingerprints in Gould's office.   .....

    d He knows something about religion.   .....

    e He knows exactly who he wants to kill and why.   .....

After you read

19 Discuss with another student:

    a the difference between Mills's ideas about the killer and
      Somerset's.

    b Somerset's reason for wanting to retire.

    c the relationship between Dworkin's past and the word SLOTH
      on the wall above the bed.

    d the importance of Mills's feelings about the night Rick got
      shot.

20 Why does Somerset take Mills to the public library? What does
he discover there?

Chapters 4–5

Before you read

21 Read the title of Chapter 4 and look at the picture on page 31.
Who is John Doe, and is that his real name? What are Somerset
and Mills doing?

22 Do you think the detectives are getting closer to catching the killer? Why (not)?

While you read

23 Answer these questions with Yes or No.
    a Does John Doe shoot at Mills and Somerset?   .....
    b Does Mills catch Doe in the apartment?   .....
    c Does Doe shoot Mills?   .....
    d Does Somerset call an ambulance?   .....
    e Does Doe take the bullets out of Mills's gun and throw them at Mills?   .....
    f Do the detectives find photographs of Doe's victims in Doe's apartment?   .....
    g Does Doe return to his apartment?   .....

24 Write the correct word on the line.

(a) .... phones Somerset after midnight. When she meets him the next morning, she tells him that she does not feel **(b)** .... in the city or in her own home. She is going to have a **(c)** .... but she is afraid. She thinks that maybe she shouldn't keep the baby. Somerset tells her to never tell **(d)** .... if she decides not to keep it. When Somerset returns to the precinct house, he hears about the killer's next **(e)** ....

After you read

25 In your opinion, why does Doe:
    a let Mills live?
    b have photos of Somerset and Mills at Dworkin's apartment?
    c phone his apartment when Somerset and Mills are there?
    d have to change his plans?
    e have thousands of notebooks?
    f have a photo of a blonde woman standing on a street corner?

26 Answer these questions.

   a Who is the victim at the next murder scene?

   b Why does Mills feel angry when he sees the dead woman's blonde hair?

   c What did Doe do to the man?

   d Which of the seven deadly sins was the murderer thinking of?

   e Why does the man cry?

Chapters 6–7

Before you read

27 There are three more deadly sins left: envy, wrath, and pride. What kind of person does John Doe plan to kill for these sins, do you think? Will the detectives be able to stop him before he kills more people? Why (not)?

28 What will Tracy do? Will she tell David about the baby or will she decide not to keep it? Why?

29 Look at the pictures on pages 39, 45, and 47. What is happening, do you think?

While you read

30 What happens next? Circle the correct choice.

   a Who phones Mills at 4:38 in the morning?

      1) Somerset   **3)** the officer guarding Doe's apartment

      2) Doe

   b What does Doe do to the beautiful woman?

      1) He drugs her.   **2)** He saves her.   **3)** He cuts off her nose.

   c How does the woman die?

      1) She kills herself.   **3)** Doe makes her take pills.

      2) She loses too much blood.

   d When Doe arrives at the precinct house, he

      1) uses his gun   **2)** holds up his hands   **3)** shouts angrily

   e While Doe talks to his lawyer, Somerset suggests that

      1) they should question him

      2) the murders have stopped

      3) there will be two more dead bodies

31 Match the names with the descriptions. Write 1–5.

    a Mark Swarr   .....

    b Doe   .....

    c Somerset   .....

    d Mills   .....

    e California   .....

        1) drives Doe into the desert and stops the car

        2) delivers Doe's message to the detectives about his last two victims

        3) sits in the helicopter listening to Somerset and Mills

        4) stays with Doe while Somerset runs toward the van

        5) will plead madness if Mills and Somerset do not agree to his plan

32 Write the correct name.

    a Who does John Doe envy?   ....

    b Who thinks there is a bomb in the box?   ....

    c Who wishes for a simple life?   ....

    d Who tells Mills to throw down his gun?   ....

    e Whose head is in the box?   ....

After you read

33 Who says these things and why?

    a "I tried to play husband. Tried to be a simple man ... but it didn't work."

    b "Murder a suspect, Mills, and you throw everything away."

    c "OK ... he wins."

    d "We'll get him a good lawyer, but he'll go to prison."

    e "I've changed my mind. I'm staying."

34 Answer these questions about Doe. Why does he:

    a say he admire Mills and Somerset?

    b say that he will plead madness?

    c envy Mills?

    d kill Tracy?

    e want Mills to shoot him?

35 Has Doe won? Why (not)?

Writing

36 Imagine that Somerset is visiting Mills in prison shortly after he kills Doe. Write a conversation between the two detectives.

37 Somerset says, "People used to kill somebody for a purpose. Now they do it for the hell of it, just to see what will happen." Do you agree with Somerset? Why (not)?

38 Why did Doe do the things that he did? Was he mad or not?

39 Imagine that you write for a newspaper. Write a news report about the death of one of Doe's victims.

40 Detective Somerset writes a letter to the local newspaper. He wants people to understand why Mills killed Doe. Does he believe that Mills should go to prison for many years? Write his letter.

41 Write about the two detectives in this book. Describe and compare their characters and their attitudes toward their work.

42 Imagine you are Mills. Write a letter from prison to your old friend Rick. Tell him about John Doe and Tracy, and describe how you feel. Are you sorry that you shot Doe or not? Do you still want to be a policeman after you leave prison? Why (not)?

43 Which character in the story do you feel most sorry for? Why? Explain.

44 Do you like this story? Why (not)? Write a letter to a friend giving your opinion of it.

45 Doe kept thousands of notebooks. What were his feelings about the seven deadly sins? Choose one and write Doe's opinion of people who are guilty of this sin.

WORD LIST

anymore (adv) any longer (time)

bandage (n/v) a piece of cloth that you tie around a part of the body that is hurt

blond (adj) with very light colored hair

client (n) a person who gets services or advice from a professional person or organization

clue (n) a piece of information that helps someone to solve a crime

cop (n) police officer (informal)

darkroom (n) a dark room where photographers print pictures from photographic film

doorman (n) a man whose job is to stand at the door of a building

evidence (n) information that is used in a court of law to prove that someone is guilty or not guilty

freeway (n) a very wide road in the US, built for fast travel

heavy-metal (n) a type of rock music with a strong beat, played very loudly on electric guitars

helicopter (n) a flying machine that can fly in all directions and can also stay still in the air

homicide (n) murder

investigation (n) trying to find out the truth about something, such as a crime

kneel (v) to rest your body on your knees; the past form is **knelt**

link (n) a connection between two ideas or things

massage parlor (n) a place where people pay to receive sexual services

neat (adj) tidy and carefully organized

nod (v) to move your head up and down to mean Yes

obvious (adj) very easy to notice or understand

plead (v) (1) to say formally in a court of law that you are guilty or innocent; (2) to request something very strongly and emotionally

precinct (n) the main police station in an area of a US city

retire (v) to stop working, usually when you have reached a certain age

row (n) a line of things

serial killer (n) a person who kills several times

sin (n) an action that is against religious rules and an offence against God

somehow (adv) for some reason

spaghetti (n) a type of food from Italy

suspect (n) a person who the police think may be guilty of a crime

victim (n) a person who suffers as a result of a crime

The Canterville Ghost and Other Stories
Oscar Wilde

The famous Canterville Ghost haunts an old house, but the ghost becomes unhappy when the new owners play tricks on *him*! In the other stories, we meet Lord Arthur Savile, who has to murder someone before he can get married, and we discover the secret life of beautiful Lady Alroy.

Love Actually
Richard Curtis

In London, Christmas is coming and the people in this story have love on their minds. Some have found love; some have lost it. Some accept their loneliness; others live in hope. Even the new British prime minister's thoughts are not always on his job – because love, actually, is all around us.

The Time Machine
H. G. Wells

The Time Traveller has built a time machine and has gone into the future to the year 802,701. He expects to find a better world with highly intelligent people and great inventions. Instead, he finds that people have become weak, child-like creatures. They dance and sing and wear flowers. They seem happy, but why are they so frightened of the dark? And who or what has taken his time machine? Will the Time Traveller ever be able to return to the present?

There are hundreds of Penguin Readers to choose from – world classics, film adaptations, modern-day crime and adventure, short stories, biographies, American classics, non-fiction, plays ...

For a complete list of all Penguin Readers titles, please contact your local Pearson Longman office or visit our website.

The Picture of Dorian Gray
Oscar Wilde

An artist paints a picture of the young and handsome Dorian Gray. When he sees it, Dorian makes a wish that changes his life. As he grows older, his face stays young and handsome. But the picture changes. Why can't Dorian show it to anybody? What is its terrible secret?

Three Adventures of Sherlock Holmes
Sir Arthur Conan Doyle

Sherlock Holmes is a great detective. There are few cases that he cannot solve. In these three stories we meet a young woman who is very frightened of a 'speckled band', a family who think that five orange pips are a sign of death, and a banker who believes that his son is a thief. But are things really as they seem?

The Client
John Grisham

Mark Sway is eleven and he knows a terrible secret. He knows where a body is hidden. Some secrets are so dangerous that it's better not to tell. But it's just as dangerous if you don't. So Mark needs help fast . . . because there isn't much time.

There are hundreds of Penguin Readers to choose from – world classics, film adaptations, modern-day crime and adventure, short stories, biographies, American classics, non-fiction, plays ...

For a complete list of all Penguin Readers titles, please contact your local Pearson Longman office or visit our website.

www.penguinreaders.com

Longman Dictionaries

Express yourself with confidence!

Longman has led the way in ELT dictionaries since 1935. We constantly talk to students and teachers around the world to find out what they need from a learner's dictionary.

Why choose a Longman dictionary?

Easy to understand

Longman invented the Defining Vocabulary – 2000 of the most common words which are used to write the definitions in our dictionaries. So Longman definitions are always clear and easy to understand.

Real, natural English

All Longman dictionaries contain natural examples taken from real-life that help explain the meaning of a word and show you how to use it in context.

Avoid common mistakes

Longman dictionaries are written specially for learners, and we make sure that you get all the help you need to avoid common mistakes. We analyse typical learners' mistakes and include notes on how to avoid them.

Innovative CD-ROMs

Longman are leaders in dictionary CD-ROM innovation. Did you know that a dictionary CD-ROM includes features to help improve your pronunciation, help you practice for exams and improve your writing skills?

**For details of all Longman dictionaries, and to choose
the one that's right for you, visit our website:**

www.longman.com/dictionaries